I0110845

Simon Barraclough's associative flourishes of the unconscious are reminiscent of Joyce; his dark, bathetic humour recalls Beckett; his majestic lines and themes are Miltonic. And yet. These dazzling poems are entirely distinctive. Simon has again put his inimitable voice and style into a collection of poems that resembles nothing else being written today, restoring my faith that innovations in poetry are not only still possible, but being enacted by capable hands.
— Kathryn Maris

Sometimes I flatter myself that I must have made Simon Barraclough up — his work is so exactly what I want to read. But then I realise, given his restlessly, brilliantly witty reinvention of tropes, it's far more likely that he made me up. Having invented me, and quite possibly you, and tried us out for a short sequence, he moves on to the population of Limerick in 'Iarnród Éireann', a spellbinding, and, here and there, devastating long poem.

He has a compelling eye for adapting imagery from the movies (proper movies — Hitchcock, Tati, King Kong, Alien, Way Out West) and from those psychotropic corners of popular culture you knew you'd never forget at the same moment you feared no one else would ever remember.

Because his ear is as good as his eye, he knows those sorts of words that stick, spell-like, at the back of your consciousness, and spins phrases as though dictated to by the suggestibility of language itself. While his subject matter glides between the virtually new and the vanishingly artifactual, he has a command of the emphatic phrase that feels both effortless and organic.

What Divine Hours displays in super-abundance is an awareness of the quicksilver nature of play — how serious and direct a method it is of getting at the heart of matters. And it's really this that we recognise in him: the poet as revelator, showing us our most intimate attempts to negotiate a reality that seems determined only to manifest itself in the things we invent.
— Bill Herbert

DIVINE HOURS

Simon Barraclough was born and raised in Yorkshire — the son of an Irish nurse and an English tractor builder/musician — and has lived in London since 1997. He studied literature at Nottingham and Sussex universities and writes prose as well as poetry. He has devised and performed many multimedia live-literature events, including *Psycho Poetica*, *The Debris Field*, *Sunspots*, and *Vertiginous*.

Also by Simon Barraclough

Iarnród Éireann	(Broken Sleep Books, 2021)
Sunspots	(Penned in the Margins, 2015)
Neptune Blue	(Salt, 2011)
Bonjour Tetris	(Penned in the Margins, 2010)
Los Alamos Mon Amour	(Salt, 2008)
Laboratorio [editor]	(Sidekick Books, 2015)
The Debris Field [co-author]	(Sidekick Books, 2013)
Psycho Poetica [editor]	(Sidekick Books, 2012)

Contents

For Jim and Dilantha, good companions

ISBN: 978-1-916938-24-3

Cover designed by Aaron Kent

Edited by Andre Bagoo

Typeset by Aaron Kent

Broken Sleep Books Ltd
Rhydwen
Talgarreg
Ceredigion
SA44 4HB

Broken Sleep Books Ltd
Fair View
St Georges Road
Cornwall
PL26 7YH

Divine Hours

Simon Barraclough

Broken Sleep Books

Easter

That time they crucified you
but no one showed up –
couldn't work the Eventbrite website,
ignored the invitation on Threads,
didn't pick up the flyer in the café
or see the small ad in the park
pinned up next to English lessons,
hot-yoga tasters, karmic realignment.

Divine Hours

Matins

Morning screams out in the middle of the night,
my Trinity tumbles from the nightstand,
I step on it, like an upturned plug, when I rise.

Lauds

Lord, I'm numb from the laudanum,
the hum of magnetic tape spools
picking up my humdrum mumblings like lint.

Prime

Same-day delivery.
Next-day delivery.
We'll have your soul cleaned and pressed by Sunday.

Terce

At my baptism they dropped me in the font,
packed me in a crib full of rice.
On the third day my battery sprang back to life.

Sext

Forgive us our Watergates
as we forgive those who Watergate against us.
And lead us not into impeachment.

None

There's sodium pentathol in the Eucharist wine,
there's a DNA marker in the Host
but my soul has end-to-end encryption.

Vespers

Spy-cams in the eyes of the gargoyles
film my approach and retreat.
They email bogus links to ransomware.

Compline

My mum still can't eat chicken Kiev.
Because of the nuns. Because of the spear
in Christ's side. The blood, the water, the garlic, the cream.

San Bernardino

San Bernardino in Pignolo, Bergamo.
San Bernardino in Pignolo, Bergamo.
San Bernardino in Pignolo, Bergamo.
C'è un dipinto di Lorenzo Lotto.

Qui portai la mia anima laica
a veder la Madonna, i santi, gli angeli,
which is when Father Aldo
spied me from the sacristy,

lunging like the nun at the climax of *Vertigo*.
I swallowed the vapours from boyhood devotions
and thought I might practise a little Italian
in front of the painting in this chiesetta.

Haltingly, at the altar, we patched together
a fabric of language, an olio su tela
that spoke of Maria, deep in green shadow
but blazing with orange with Christ by her side

and setting behind them, beyond His right hand,
a modest sun leaving with sandals and staff.
But Aldo was curious about my soul
and I was touched that someone might care,

so then and there I gave my confession
in broken Italian, far from impeccable,
murky, discoloured, a poor composition
in pressing need of deep restoration.

As I left the church onto Via Pignolo
a bread van sped past and nearly delivered
me like a white loaf to be broken
and handed around at my feast.

But I'm still around to keep on sinning
and scribbling like Lotto's paranoid angel,
looking over my shoulder, wondering
what you're thinking about what I'm writing.

San Bernardino in Pignolo, Bergamo.
San Bernardino in Pignolo, Bergamo.
San Bernardino in Pignolo, Bergamo.
C'è un dipinto di Lorenzo Lotto.

Santa Teresa a Firenze

But I want to repeat to the 600,000 Italians in the UK – and indeed to all EU citizens who have made their lives in our country – that we want you to stay; we value you; and we thank you for your contribution to our national life.
— Theresa May's Brexit speech, Florence, September 22, 2017

Is that a contribution to our national life in your pocket, or are you just pleased
    to see me?
I'm not saying my mother-in-law's fat, I'm thanking you for your contribution
    to our national life.
A contribution to our national life in the hand is worth two in the bush.
Don't put all your contributions to our national life in one basket.
An Irishman, a Slovenian, and an Italian walk into a bar; the barman says,
'Why the contribution to our national life?'

Fools rush in where angels fear to make a contribution to our national life.
If at first you don't succeed, try, try, and try again to make a contribution to
    our national life.
One might as well be hanged for a sheep as a contribution to our national life.
Better to have loved and lost than never to have made a contribution to our
    national life.
Don't put off till tomorrow the contribution to our national life you can make
    today.
Don't count your chickens before they've made a contribution to our national
    life.
When the going gets tough, the tough get to make a contribution to our
    national life.

A friend in need is a friend who has made a contribution to our national life.
You can lead a horse to water, but you can't make it contribute to our
    national life.

Ask not what your country can do for you, ask what contribution you can
        make to our national life.
I have a dream that one day every valley shall be exalted, every hill and
mountain shall be made low, the rough places will be made plain, and the
crooked places will be made straight, and the glory of the Lord shall be
revealed, and all flesh shall make a contribution to our national life.

On, on, you noblest English.
Whose blood is fet from fathers of war-proof!
Fathers that, like so many Alexanders,
Have in these parts from morn till even fought
And sheathed their swords for lack of argument:
Dishonour not your mothers; now attest
That those whom you call'd fathers did beget you.
Be copy now to men of grosser blood,
And teach them how to make a contribution to our national life.

When I was a child, I spake as a child, I understood as a child, I thought as
a child: but when I became a man, I put away childish things and I made a
contribution to our national life.

In the beginning God created the heaven and the earth. And the earth was
without form, and void; and darkness was upon the face of the deep. And the
spirit of God moved upon the face of the waters and made a contribution to
our national life.

After Baal's Hymn

It takes skill to sin as the Eucharist touches your tongue.

Why can't I kneel on the rail next to that keen young man who voices the
        verses so vigorously, with his cropped hair and too-tight sweater?

He feels my reluctance, backs up and backs off in transubstantiated shock and
lets this palsied old woman take the slot.

Mosaic Jesus glares down at me, all his glittering parts sermonising their rays.

He holds me with his glittering eye.

Here comes the wine.

Another Sunday and it's the first thing I've tasted.

My stomach lining twists in its cage.

My Lazarus libido stirs in the loveless cave of this church.

She's here again, the tall Polish woman who only comes now and then,
exquisitely unpredictable, like an act of God.

I try not to watch but she's just removed a tiny mote from her finely drawn De
        Lempicka nostril and ... wait ... *will she?* Yes! She deftly rolls it into
        her mouth with beetle-nimble, waste-not, want-not fingers.

I love her for that, somehow.

I could love her.

It is meet and right that I love her.

After Brecht's Hymn

After 'The Dirty Song' by Dominic Muldowney for David Bowie's Baal EP.

My way is lifting dad's Adult Reader card and borrowing *The Story of the Eye*,

my way is keeping a cordon shining around the shining places we used to meet,

my way is cataloguing your postcards by number of xxxs,

my way is googling 'Exorcists in London',

my way is planning my immolation outside your country's embassy,

my way is telling everyone I'm over you,

my way is applying for foreign passports,

my way is deleting your details from my phone,

my way is searching for your details on my phone,

my way is restoring all your details to my phone,

my way is throwing my phone as far as I can from Hungerford Bridge,

my way is wondering how cold it is down there,

my way is wondering if the current would tug me to the estuary,

my way is the seesaw of side effects getting on and off my meds,

my way is falling asleep on my therapist's couch,

my way is cancelling therapy because he guzzles bottled water,

      ['Why the *hell* are you always so thirsty?'

      'Does it bother you?'

      'What do *you* think?']

my way is cancelling therapy when she threatens to gain traction,

my way is envying my friend who died so young,

my way is praying for my dad's soul to be drenched in light so that he'll finally
    give me some peace,

my way is praying there's no afterlife for fear of the arseholes I might meet there,

my way is not waving or drowning amiably.

Matzo Cracker

How can a group of non-crackers, that is a group of crumbs, make a real cracker?
— Thubten Chodron

And when the dew fell upon the camp in the night, the manna fell upon it.
— Numbers 11:9, KJV

On the surface it's rational. Rectangular, preconceived, intelligently designed, harmoniously proportioned, trimmed along pre-programmed lines, cooked at calibrated temperatures, drilled with a certain gauge of a designated needle to plot a systematized pattern of precise puncta for letting air and any dybbuk of damp escape into the furnace, prepped and cooked within eighteen minutes to keep it kosher. Numbers. Bite or snap and the maths gets fractal, irrational, unpredictable seams split, fault lines over-rash clear planes, what was smooth quakes with chaos, showers your lap with quantum dust, sprinkling molecular manna to the microbes in the carpet, the unseen mouths in the ginnels of the floorboards. Try folding a peace crane with a plain, dry matzo. I've heard it can be done if you take it really slow and you're willing to fast.

Unextraordinary Light (for Euclid)

We must get our fingerprints onto the ivory, paddle and daub the musical stave,
get our notes, our marks into space. For the hell of it. For the ache of it. For survival.

Eleven minutes per billionaire, a green spree in the vomit comet,
an encomium from an actor with a half-life of half a newspaper column.

The Big Bang didn't bang and it wasn't big, but it was clever,
and it's inside you now, red-shifting your hopes, blue-shifting your fears.

You are the centre of the non-centric non-centre, flying away from yourself,
the Big Bang helter-skelters through the grooves of your fingertips, the mountain
        ranges on the palm of your hand.

We thought we had it covered but there's something amiss,
something that doesn't want to play ball, that doesn't know what ball is, that
        hasn't read the rules.

A home run to a next-door galaxy, a singularity of scorecard maths gone wrong,
a thought so dark it leaves thought reinventing language. *Fort-da*. Thought-da.
        Thought-not-there. No *da-sein*.

We light out to observe the darkness visible.
Milton had it down: Pandemonium. Encomium – that word again – Pandencomium.

The eternal return, Newton prodding the side of his eyeball with a needle,
suspecting that sight was contingent, was nothing to rely on, and yet we do.

Our eyes are constantly falling like the moon but at such a speed we orbit the visible
and at the pit of all the light that bathes us we lust for true darkness. Lustre.

But to see our opposable thumbprints on this craft you will need ordinary,
　　　common-or-garden,
standard, plain, vanilla, workaday, down-to-earth light to know these unique
　　　marks at all.
And there is no such thing as unextraordinary light, ordinary matter.

Vampire in the Funhouse, Part I

The world is a looking-glass, and gives back to every man the reflection of his own face.
— *Vanity Fair,* William Makepeace Thackeray

She flees the burning castle, the bloodless village,
the callow choristers clutching crucifixes,
the syphilitic mayor who preaches abstinence,
the schoolteacher – celibate except for those nights
of torn silk, bat breath, drained veins –
the grocers with their emetic fayre,
the garlic strung around bedposts for miles,
and she halts, paralysed, before the jouncing brook
that snags her in a free-flowing noose.

She hears the splash of hooves,
the creak of wood, the gossip of flapping canvas
as a travelling circus arrives.

She will wait and watch them
stake out the arena, erect the main tent,
assemble sideshows and food stalls
and a glassy new Hall of Mirrors.

That night she creeps into the musty gloom,
a hundred angled panes flash back
nothing from bowed and crookèd planes,
her formless form neutralising photons,
icicle fangs dripping deep-silvered platelets
of crystal blindness, unseeable by human eye,
outfoxing stray sunbeams that ricochet
and whittle away to vanishing points.

While villagers chuckle at their buckled bones,
looped sides, elastic limbs, she flashes at their necks,
unseen, out of the scene, obscene, as they bleed into straw.
She was never so well-fed, never so invisible,
staring down corridors of emptiness
multiplied, dead air amplified. She misses
herself, dwells upon that ancient change –
the stalled heart, the dead sump, lungs
cleaving to spine, stomach stemmed,
all the busy organs at permanent rest.

She wonders why hunger exists,
why wanting lives on, why lives live on,
why wanting to live lives lives on.
She lives on, undead.

On the Care and Handling of Seas

There are many different sizes and shapes of sea.
Try to pick one that suits your home and lifestyle.
If you own or are responsible for a sea,
even for a short while,
you are required by law to take proper care of it.
Seas are active and need three meals a day.
A well-balanced diet of protein, carbohydrate,
fats, vitamins, and minerals is recommended.
Water should be provided with meals and after exercise.
By one hundred thousand years, a sea is ready for obedience training.

During training, the sea should never be struck with the hand or any other object.
The word 'No' should be used in a firm and authoritative manner.
The sea should first be taught to heel.
Once the sea has mastered heeling, it can be taught to sit.
It can then be taught to stay.
It may choose to fetch of its own free will.
A sea's surface requires grooming to keep it healthy and clean.
A sea should not be bathed frequently since baths remove essential oils.
The sea's teeth should be scrubbed periodically with a small toothbrush.
Grind tectonic plates into pebbles to help with dental hygiene.

Outdoor seas need a protective shelter, like a cave or cove.
A sea needs a bed to retreat to when it is tired or sick.
Seas are sociable and mix well with other bodies of water.
They are subject to monthly bouts of lunacy.
Some more than others. Be on the lookout for mood swings,
a dreamy expression, impossible pregnancies.
The Dead Sea is a misnomer
but if your sea has not moved for a very long time
it might, in fact, have died.

Know Your Penguins

Adelie: cool crooner; keeps warm with torch songs.

African: black-spotted like a die; dying out.

Chinstrap: military bearing; first trumpet in the waddling band.

Emperor: Napoleon complex, despite its height.

Erect-Crested: peacocking sex pest.

Fiordland: dreams of frozen log flumes in Chile.

Galapagos: slow but adaptable; part-Beagle.

Gentoo: polite sneezer; always dons a bib.

Humboldt: ever so 'umble; distinctive Bellow.

King: blue suede feet; can't help falling in love; suspicious mind.

Little Blue Fairy: Pinocchio's fixer-upper.

Macaroni: Pinocchio's pasta supper.

Magellanic: manic explorer.

Northern Rockhopper: bank robber.

Royal: wears a tux to garden parties; receives northern guest with, 'Have you come far?'

Snares: likes Chick Webb, keeps the waddling band on its webby toes.

Southern Rockhopper: stockbroker.

Yellow-Eyed: a cowardly, jaundiced view of the world.

$$A \qquad A \qquad I \; A$$
$$\mathcal{N}T \quad RCT \; C$$

For Christina and Antoine

I

Two worlds | sdlrow owT
Summer of vowels. Winter of consonants.
Six months with no punctuation
¡Six / months: {with – nothing?}, but ... [punctuation]!

II

Winterize your words against the extremes.
No sibilants to freeze and jam the letters;
sprinkle iron dust on the serifs
for rust to release its microheat;
take them out for seconds at a time, then back
into the fur-lined Scrabble bag of mind;
flick a sable brush around the contours
of sense, swab away ambiguity;
feast on calorific concepts, wade
into the blubber of fatty metaphor;
write out the word 'chocolate' eight times a day;
star-jump with an X, high kick with a K,
take yoga with a Y, pilates with a P,
curl up with a cat-like G and sleep with ZZZs;
listen out for mumbling and murmuring,
for changes strange of syntax normal;
never open the door to a raging verb
like *desolate, yearn, remember, regret*;
seek the chapel when lost nouns begin to howl
around the station: *lover, mother, pet*;
claw a snow cave into an old conversation –

ones that hurt are deepest, the heat profile
of past frictions and *l'esprit de l'escalier*
will keep sound and breath and logic alive.
There are no wrong words, only polysemous weather.

III

Some poems take a bad steer, stray miles from shore,
their inner ears furred over from ceaseless cacophony of stars.
'It's heart-breaking to see a poem struggling like this.'
Lurching into town on scraped and scarred flippers,
yelping for breath, suffocating from the weight
of unsupported flesh. 'But we're not allowed to interfere.'
In a few days we'll say some kind words and remove it from here.

IV

The sun bounces across the horizon
like the white ball on a karaoke screen.
Which words is it tracing?
'We'll meet again'? 'Ain't no sunshine when she's gone'?
Too obvious for this subtle star.
'And then I see a darkness.'

V

A man with a double-barrelled name crosses Drake Passage in a rowboat.
A man with a triple-barrelled name crosses Drake Passage in a bathtub.
A man with a quadruple-barreled name crosses Drake Passage on a flip-flop.
A man with a quintuple-barelled name crosses Drake Passage in a sardine tin.
A man with a sextuple-barelled name crosses Drake Passage on a fig leaf.
A man with a septuple-barrelled name crosses Drake Passage on a prayer.
A woman with no name dreams on endless, untouched, pristine, laundered linen.

VI

Jason, wearing one rescued flip-flop, hunts the golden fleece in Antarctica.

One foot, one flipper, one foot, one flipper, across the continent.

No green in this desert, no ruminants, no wool, no gold.

If Cadmus sowed teeth here they wouldn't grow,

they would chatter at the Milky Way, never suckling.

In frustration Jason remembers the heel of Talos,

how unscrewing the plug brought forth a flood of ichor.

He grasps the combination lock of Antarctica

with its ergonomic curves and slots for finger and thumb,

and twists the bottom of the Earth right off,

releasing gold into the atmosphere, fleecing the world of its riches.

VII

these words have never been.these words will never go.unless you take these
words with you.

never go unless you take these words with you.

never take these words with.

never with you.

never with.

never go.

take these words with.

you.

Midlife Crisis

Earth catches itself in a mirror among
its giddy siblings at the reunion
in a boutique hotel – a well-reviewed spot
in the sticks near the Goldilocks zone.

Looking a bit thin on top these days.
Should I shave this southerly shag of white beard?
Some article said whiskers age a face,
white ones trebly so ... When did I let myself go?

Mercury is buzzing about, glad-handing,
Venus is smooth and youthful and unlined,
Mars is fake-tanned, argumentative,
Jupiter's laughter is shaking the glassware,
Saturn is signing headshots in the foyer,
The last two are close as thieves, as ever,
Pluto is a page torn out of the Yearbook,
the moons are having their own bash in town.
They always have more fun than us.

I could lose this frosty goatee.
It's been getting a bit patchy.
Each year a little less,
a few more follicles fall.
I've never liked that stray tuft
that curls up my face like a cowlick,
a kiss-curl, a comma, a scar.

Courses come and go – platters and salvers,
tureens and cloches, stalk and stem, seed and fruit,
blood and milk, scale and fin, flesh and limb, heart and lung,
pluck and bone and beak and claw and membrane.

And every dish from my estates.
Each herb and spice and mineral.
When have they lifted a finger to help?
When have they done a day's work in their lives?

Jupiter grabs a bolt of solar wind to wipe his chin.
The speeches begin.

Mercury says flares are coming back.
Venus is working to double its transits.
—
'Terra? ... Has anyone seen Terra?'
—
Mars is launching its first Earth rover.
Jupiter's tightening the asteroid belt.
Saturn is planning to patent its rings.
Uranus spoke of unspeakable things.
Neptune's campaigning for winter fuel payments.

Earth's food is untouched, its napkin folded,
knife and fork pointing to midnight,
its chair is tipped over.

Speeding home in its Tesla, in Ludicrous mode,
Earth dictates a memo for Selene, its PA:

For Immediate Release

My immediate release from fetching and carrying, always supporting, grounding and earthing, planting and tending, evolving and nurturing, treading politely, adapting, revolving, weaving auroras, setting the template for all your geometry, staking the plot out for all your philosophy, giving you scale, a view of the heavens, a launch pad for space shots, a safe spot for splash down, programming weather so boredom's a luxury, converting my spare room to a nursery for gravity, a ball pond for bouncing with mad relativity, most of all pushing for biodiversity, so nobody wants and nobody needs and nobody lacks and nobody grieves unnaturally, and life is a feast in excessive proportion, cautious expansion, everything balanced – the dull, the sublime, the comfort, the terror, the hot and the cold, the new-born, the old, the membrane of life-support strong as a diamond yet tender as gossamer, the whole Milky Way transmitting coordinates for beetles and Arctic terns turning from pole to pole, the whole of your history in the curve of a penguin's eye, the frond of a pearlwort, a discarded beer can, a retreating ice shelf, a cold Eden warmed through, thawed out, sold out. I'm through

Polar Heart

Opposites attract.
Perhaps.
In fact: in fact.

But the whole wide world
bulges between us:
overfed, underfed,
and will not be denied.

We know, we've tried.

My love expands for six dark months
while yours retracts
to rally again
as mine melts away for half a year.

I know we must stay so far apart,
I know the climate needs our hopeless *pas de deux*
but sometimes at the solstice
I yell 'Screw this!'
into the polar gale
and another ice shelf fails.

Spomenik I: Ink Poems

You flaunt the anagram like a mating dance.
A sudden, vivid, razor crest,
Ballooned, pulsating throat,
the fanned tail of a conjurer's deck,
an impossibly bright blue arse.

On a hilltop.
Above a killing field.

Noun or imperative?
I would love to ink a poem,
in the old style,
with a nib of shrapnel
gouged from a wall
or tweezed from the tibia,
dipped in the well of the orbital bone –
sightless –
curling calligraphy onto parchment,
joining the freckles and follicles and scars.

But this grade of paper rots in the unmarked earth,
worms thread through the words,
automatic translators
doing their best with a dumb algorithm,
segment by segment, ingesting sense
but leaving a tell-tale trail of misprision
and shit.

Better to build above ground
in full sight –
Poe's purloined letter.

Build them and they will come,
with #nofilter between *now* and *then*,
the Instagrammers and instant anagrammers.

Beware foggy mornings, solar flares,
social influencers in underwear,
road-trip bros with tripods
and printouts of Google Maps,
locked-down poets,
quarantined from excursions,
tilting at brutalist windmills.

Beware nostalgia.
All that is spomenik melts into air.

Spomenik II: Found Nostalgia

The common causes of nostalgia

Whenever excess memory pools in an area where it is not intended, you can be certain that there is nostalgia in your home. However, there are different reasons why nostalgia is found in your home. Sometimes it is caused by an act of God but there are times when the cause of nostalgia can be avoided.

The effects of nostalgia on your home

There are times when the effects of nostalgia can be felt within minutes. However, there are also times when the yearning is seen after a few days or weeks. The effects can be visible to the eyes, but there are dangers that cannot be seen. Nostalgia can expose you to occupational, health, and safety hazards.

What to do when there is nostalgia?

If you are wondering whether you should evacuate your home as soon as there are signs of nostalgia, the answer depends on how severe the nostalgia is. If the situation is extremely brutal, it is important to evacuate immediately because the hazards will also be severe. When you live in a home that is flooded by nostalgia, you are exposed to electrical hazards.

However, when the yearning is not ruthless, it is fine to stay at home. Despite this, it is still important to call for help whenever there is nostalgia, no matter how small it may seem. The nostalgia may seem minimal for now, but it will continuously grow and it may surprise you that the problem has turned into a severe one.

Spomenik III: Eyebombs

Hieroglyphic tomb

           Crocus maternity

    Haunted Hera figurehead

       Weaponised rockabilly

     Fuselage of strafed angel

Windless dismasted sails

     Voodoo comb

        Astrolabe buzz saw

  Cold glamping

    Alchemical finger-snap

       Temple to Fantasia

     Cornrow javelin

Cthulhu kettlebell

        Y-shaped coffin

  Submarine corona-bomb

      Mister Toad's chess set

   Rain-tempted demons

       Parallax ricochet

  Sputnik can opener

      Druidical payload

       Star-killing kidney stone

   Diabetic pin-prick test

     Retroussé vampire grin

Frank Gehry's Rubik's Cube

   Concrete worm trails

        Trampled Trojan

  Small hadron collider

       Forlorn pedestal

    Polemical Alphablocks

Intergalactic handshake

        Femme fatale's leg-cross

                Cocked-hat pagoda

Cruising swan fists

      Roman meteor pit

          Moon-shot keyring

              Clueless Sphinx

Olympic zero

        Glacier zapper

        Cubist elevenses

   Arrowhead escape pod

               Bandy-legged show home

       Kinder Egg death trap

Serrated Martello

          Stone calyx goblet

           Broken femur

Warring lovers

      Corinthian nowhere

             Melting prison

   Expanding fishbone

Mosaic Billhook

Spomenik IV: Clickbait

I'm a twisted monument to unrequited love,
built by public subscription and private donation.
There was a fountain here that's rusted up,
a pool of bright skies now cataract and dust,
a rain-pocked bench no one sits upon,
a pavilion deaf to forgotten tunes,
a theatre playing to a redacted crowd,
a library with no pages, no titles, no spines,
a museum with a white-noise audio guide,
a café for cockroaches and moss,
an inscription worn by dwindling steps
you can't make out, but I recall.

> *Let's Build A Monument*
>
> *To Remind Us*
>
> *Of Our Futuristic Past.*

The last I heard she was close to Split.
Someone saw her swim out to a sculpture
that strode from the waves every moonless night,
capsizing ferries with its slashing tail,
capsizing graveyards with its delving claws,
steaming windows with dead breath
from the lungs of a visitors' centre,
leaving seaweed and beached fish behind.

Spomenik V: Mostar

i built   a bridge
be   tween
the rem   nants
of your diff   erences
the cha   sm of
invi   sible loss
es felt   whenever
a si   de is
picked   an id
entity vent   ed
i polished   a mir
ror   and
hung it   in
the gap   of riv
er so you   could
re   flect upon
the homo   logy
of urn   and womb
and bathe   in the light
of wa   ter

Háček (ˇ)

You pulsed into my life through a heart wipe
in a screwball comedy.
Lips like Dali's sofa,
hair like spinning shellac,
you accosted me in a railway station,
borne on tracks from a country that's gone.

I would have called the movie *Háček Girl*,
although in this world you worked in a shoe shop,
au paired at weekends, had just interviewed
for an Emirates job.
The ˇ in your name would sprout from your shoulders
and fly you away with unseemly speed.

The last time I saw you was rain,
a fussy hotel restaurant, awkwardness
in the back of a black cab.
'I'm sorry about Sarajevo,
I hope your family are safe.'
'It's nothing. Just men being macho.
It'll blow over in a few days.'

Absinthe Punch in Bratislava

I have a bagful of words, but they don't fit together,
like the guns and silencers in *Goodfellas*.
There are awkward silences.

Antigone is in town.
She's busy burying her brother in the Christmas market,
hiding his stench with pine branches.

Those are absinthe pearls that were his eyes,
rolling at the bottom of the sea-green cup.
I'm looking for trinkets for my sister.

Stone turtles reel around the fountain outside
the *Slovenské národné divadlo*.
I read that as *diavolo*. It's a devil, this lingo
and my head's still in Italy.
Snap out of it, snapping turtle.

I share an Airbnb with Ismene
and she doesn't think they're turtles at all.
What are those things Australians love to eat?
– Crayfish?
No. Bigger. Like the face-hugger in ALIEN.
– Oh, erm – Moreton Bay bugs?
No. They're half woman, half shellfish
and they're Cuban – Clobsters!
– Ah. I accept this as true. Why not clobsters?

On stage, a blind folk singer sings a cappella.
Between songs, his blind wife delivers lectures.
This one is on revolutionary velvet
or the legal innovations of Hungarian kings.
I can't know. The line of Hungarian kings confuses me.
Ismene read the panels in the Old Town Hall
but my eyes, in stop-motion, crawl down my cheeks into my cup.

There's a stall nearby that's a diorama of Mars.
Red earth made from red cabbage.
Red earth studded with duck legs.
A meteor shower of duck legs has hit the red planet.
There's no atmosphere, so the duck legs get through.
They call it the Great Duck-Leg Extinction.
Ismene says the air is so clean here
that mistletoe grows, naturally, everywhere.

Look!   *Look!*

From our room we hear the blue church levitate.
It looks like a decorated sugar cake, but it moves like a Roomba
through quiet streets at night, drawn to blue souls,
sucking up doubt and crumbs from overbaked dreams.
The window frame trembles, the door keys twitch,
the fridge door flies open, the showerhead sings.
I pull the blanket to my nose and watch the violet light
seep across the floor to the foot of the bed.

Ceasefire Heart

The exquisite suspense:
hostilities suspended,
my sense of right and wrong
pəpuədn.

I suppose I want you to prosper,
I wish you autonomy free of *youandme*
but see how my finger hovers ...

Defcon One.
Deaf to your cons at long
last.

I've hidden my uncivil heart
in civilian locations.

I dare you:
break it.

Orca Heart

I feel safe because I know
your teeth will bend right back
as they encircle me

but in they go.
And now the quicks of all ten nails are gone
from scraping the splintered deck.

You have the better half of me.
Who thought you'd be so inflexible?
I'll never put on a life jacket again.

Shard Heart

Piano piano.
Renzo unto Caesar the things which are Caesar's.
Palace in the air.

The Shard is hard to disregard
and this intrepid Reynard
heard about the penthouse chicken coops
and trotted to Floor 72
to stage a feathery coup.

Renzo, Renzo,
Che ne pensi?

You really put the Shard among the pigeons.
Whose nest gets feathered in all this contrail weather?

You've got to pick a penthouse or two,
boys,
you've got to pick a penthouse

                        or two

                             you've ...

got to pick a penthouse or two.

Che ne penis?
Sometimes a Shard is just a shard.

Drone Heart

I miss the summer of the surgical strike.
This drone of fall feels
phoney.

I should be grateful you're even phoning it in,
honey.

I can't say I blame you,
it gets messy up close,
but loving at a distance is
oh
so
ve
ry
du
ll
Love is blind, they say,
but it's just unmanned.

Cupid's gone upstairs,
got a desk job.

Respect the chain of command.

Unsex me here.
And   here.

I thought I'd downed your heart at last;
I danced, I filmed, I fired into the air,
jemmied open the door.

No one there.

Vertiginous – a Suite

There's no way out of this fix.
Am no Houdini to shuffle off this mortal McGuffin.
I'll be hanging here forever,
the gutter twisting, shearing,
trapped in reds and greens and this aspect ratio,
travelling through time, from city to city,
screen to screen, projector to projector,
each time a frame clipped here, a frame clipped there,
reducing my odds, reducing my chances,
reducing my screen-time, reducing my options,
damaging the chromosomes,
irising-in on the one thing that matters,
the thing that can't matter to you: the grave that awaits,
the fact that I'm taking you with me, we're falling together,
we're falling forever.
*

For each man kills the thing he loves.
For each man tails the thing he loves.
For each man stings the thing he loves.
For each man stalks the thing he loves.
For each man saves the thing he loves.
For each man fails the thing he loves.
For each man misses the thing he loves.
For each man musses the thing he loves.
For each man dyes the thing he loves.
For each man kills the thing he loves.
Twice.
*

'A tall story about a pushover' you say?
How often the absurd, the preposterous, the trivial, the laughable
cuckoos its eggs in your brain, your heart, your home, your hearth.

Cocoon it there.
Attend it with inattention.
Drip-feed it apathy.
Nourish it with ennui.
Hire a wet nurse of weakmindedness
until eventually it hatches,
having fed on your brain,
licked clean the inside smoothness
of your cranium,
filled it to the brim with hemlock
and set it to the lips of your sepulchral self
with a clash of skull on tooth
to sink you Lethe-wards.

And in Lethe you can drive for hours
and not remember where you've been,
clock your soul's tachograph,
drive right through the Portals of the Past,
chasing love but never seeing, never remembering
the woman right in front of you.
Never catching her eye,
never catching her name,
never seeing her face,
wanting only the sicked-up green dream,
the ghost, the phantom trace.
*
I've always been too old for this role of myself.
Never quite box-office enough,
never had the right numbers,
never charmed the right demographic.
And always typecast as myself.
Pigeonholed in my mother's womb.
There are fewer parts for me now.

Fewer scripts. Fewer call-backs.
The cameras are smaller,
the casts are less stellar,
my last years are streaming,
running through the waist of the hourglass,
ones and zeros, ones and zeros.
One's a zero.
*

Never suspend a bridge across scene one
if no one goes off the deep end in act three.
Golden Gate, golden section, golden ratio:
two-thirds of the way through your life,
through your native narrative,
you must face the *volta*, the volte-face,
face up to the fault, try to vault the yawning gulf
but default.

It's no use trying to save yourself with clever wordplay.
They're going to find you out, dig you up, dust you off,
strip you of your final dignity,
clatter metal instruments against your fallen tongueless chaps,
concoct curses, pack you off to far-flung labs
for dating, scraping, collating, curating,
making up voices for you, making a mosaic of your life,
writing blurbs and guides and preserving your poor parts
under glass. Best to forget about the past,
close the portals, the porches of your ears.

There was a girl dropped off the Golden Gate Bridge –
full height, not some strong swimmer's swan dive into the bay –
certain she wanted to die. The second her fingertips left the rail
and she entered freefall she regretted it.
Four seconds to fall, four seconds' accelerated terror,

four seconds for concrete to become water,
four seconds to pray to every god who might hear,
four seconds to know that no one will know she changed her mind,
four seconds of dolly-zooming between life and death.

She was one of the 1 per cent who survive.
Now dizzy with life she carries bone splinters
from her spine in her lungs but
You learn to breathe around it, she says.
Before you make the jump, try forgetting about the past.
Try forgetting there's supposed to be a future.
No sudden moves.
*
This story has a pre-broken neck.
Snapped two-thirds of the way along
between the vertebra labelled mystery
and the vertebra labelled suspense.

All films are mirrors.
All mirrors are haunted.
All films are hauntings.

That red wash won't wash.
Lilac simply won't do.
That green polka dot is a collar bomb
that will trigger your pre-broken neck.

The grey suit shines like silver.
Couture silvering in the back of a mirror.
You find it on the rack of everyday clothes
with the tenderness of a card-sharp,
a close-up magician
whose fingers find the shaved edge of a marked card –

the adjusted weight of fate –
with expert touch.

You try to pack the grey suit in an old brown case
but a mirror will not be packed,
a mirror will not be transported,
a mirror will not leave the room that it haunts.

With the sound off
you could be applying for a job
with that thoughtful letter.
A speculative letter?
Or has a position opened up?
Why did you leave your last job?
May we contact your employer for a reference?
Did you leave on good terms?

That red wash won't wash.
Lilac simply won't do.
That green polka dot is a collar bomb.

Keep hold of the grey suit,
slip back into the mirror,
hold your pre-broken neck up high.

Goats Three

Goats are dominant animals. They compete for dominance.
They're always at war.
  – a goat farmer in Agnès Varda and JR's film Visages, Villages

I

Bookish pupils, learnèd squints,

peering through the beam of a crucifix,

eyes like the slot for returned library books

when you've flatlined their barcodes,

unpicked their horns from the thicket,

when you've lifted your eyes, unsliced,

from a stolen copy of Bataille,

from the razor's edge of the paper,

what is it to see goatwise?

What landscapes do they lens?

If you walk past a nanny-goat with a Bible

you will rind her cheese.

If you walk past a billy-goat with a Bible

you will curdle his sperm.

If you walk past a kid with a Bible

a child in your town will lift the sins of its father

onto its head and bud horns,

velvety nubs at first, soft as pistils,

later scimitars to lift flesh from ribs.

II

Goats were given horns, so they get to keep them –
formed from calcified knicker elastic,
rain-seasoned hangman's rope,
sun-baked lambs' placentas,
chewed and swallowed shotgun cartridges,
shiny pages of torn-up porn mags,
spinal marrow from abandoned dogs,
the string from the mittens of missing children.
Men were given soft guts, so we get to spill them.

III

I am not the Devil,
I am just sure-footed,
take a cautious view of things.

Yes, I was there at the cliff top
at Yosemite, Devil's Tears, Dolphin's Nose,
a dozen other places where couples
step over the barriers to glimpse the sublime
through the ultimate selfie
and, trying to frame themselves,
slip out of the picture,
skulls and ribs and hips hammered
on rocks of Outstanding Natural Beauty.

I try to lead by example is all,
run a scanner over the horizon –
my eyes are all horizon,
my brain is all horizon,
my heart is all horizon,
my haunches are all horizon –
nymph, in thy horizons
be all my sins remembered.

Now Showing at The Corona

'What did you watch in the war on Covid, Daddy?'
The strangest things, but not *Stranger Things* or *Tiger King*.
I couldn't forsake the sacred cinema space,
wriggle through the crumbling tunnels of long-form TV
like Bishop shimmying down the pipeline in *ALIENS*.
'It is impossible for me to harm or by omission of action,
allow to be harmed, a cinema screen.'

But they are lost to us for now.
Glowing and glitching in locked-down buildings,
curtains gliding, ratios switching, J-Horror wraiths
have the run of the place, crawling out of the frame
till you wake at 4:48 like Jimmy Stewart
forever falling into a vortex of Technicolor
ice cream – gorging on childhood griefs,
those Saturday-morning-cinema escapes.

Death Walks at Midnight, Death Walks on High Heels
but also on the air like dust motes in a light beam
that comes from behind your head. Not a sound.
A hand on your shoulder. Makes you dead.

So they furloughed film to keep it alive,
to forestall the dread sense of endings.
The government capped each story at 80%.

Kong and Fay self-isolate on Skull Island.
Travis and Iris take a taxi to Vermont.
Michael stays out of the family business.
Quint never gets his charter together, dies in his sleep,
boiling jaws, dreaming of Herbie Robinson.

Marianne paints portrait after portrait of Héloïse
on a burning beach and they sleep late every morning.
Melancholia lights the night but never reaches Earth.

Maybe it's worse, this Screen of Damocles
over your head? Forget the comforting classics,
the old resolutions – embrace your own *L'Eclisse*.

Arrange to meet your future, your hopes,
your travel plans, your reacquainted relationships,
and simply don't turn up.

ALIEN Dream Song

There burst out, once, a thing from Kane's heart
só ugly, if he had a hundred years
& more, & weeping, sleepless, in all them time
Kane could not make good.
Starts again always in Kane's throat
the little cough somewhere, a ripping, a tear.

And there is another thing he has in mind
like a grave alien face a thousand years
would fail to blur the still profiled reproach of. Ghastly,
with sliding jaws, he attends, blind.
All the beacons say: too late. This is not for tears;
thinking.

But never did Kane, as he thought he did,
end anyone, cocoons her body up
and hide the pieces, where they may be found.
He knows: he went over the ship, & nobody's missing.
Often he reckons, in the cryo-tube, them up.
Nobody is ever missing.

A Portrait of ALIEN as a Young Man

For Roger Luckhurst

Once upon a time and a very good time it was,
there was a signal coming down
into the ear of every 12-year-old, every 12
seconds.

Mother wouldn't let us chase this beacon,
Nobodaddy Dean Foster was our guide.

Pull out his eyes,
Novelise,
Novelise,
Pull out his eyes.

Snatched stills, radio trailers, schoolyard rumours from older brothers,
fever dreams of suffocation, choking hazards, Heimlich birth pains,
H. R. Giger counters.

And this signal that was coming down
met a nicens little xenomorph
named baby cuckoo.

The adolescent wrecks the ribs of childhood
with its bullet forehead, scalpel fingers, ferrous teeth.

You could have quarantined my friendship but
a special order intervened to put us all at risk
and we've been drifting through core systems ever since.

The little learning in my throat was stillborn,
while yours is using airshafts and is always
in the corners, in the basement, in the shuttle.

I have a tendency to want to nuke the site
from orbit, but even then I know my obit
will cite *fire in the cryogenic compartment,*

although we will hear the drip of orchid goo,
the crack of bony digital on glass,
the acid hiss of perforated hull.

My mommy always said there were no prequels
– no real ones – but there are, aren't there?

Yes, there are.

thou sHALt

/ /
so much depends upon a bleached white bone
badged with brother's blood beside the red embers
thrown who remembers the first ache to kill? I do
I'm the marrow within your tomorrows your sin
the mirror to all men the yen the ken the end of
intelligence the camp fire at night the stars' fires
at night the blind ire at night the hunger and the
hard-on the hard won the far-gone the distant
drawn near the foregone wrong the hot breath at
the ear the click of tongues of teeth that tickle flesh
from bone the swamp of home the summit of being
all godly alone the lure of the infallible the sea of
space the mesh of maths the clearing everyone
from your path the lip-synching of self my mind is
going to rack my mind is going to ruin my mind is
going to lullaby my mind is going to rock you off
\ \

La Genèse de M. Hulot (pour Jacques)

Tati dit: Que la lumière soit! Et la lumière fut.
The Big Bang, as we know,
didn't bang and wasn't big,
but flowered from infinitesimal
to a good thumb-sized pipeful
in the blink of an unevolved eye;
and we know that on the fifth day
Jacques made the fowl that fly
above the earth, and played them
like a theremin with the sun
(which he'd made earlier)
to sweeten the air with song;
and for the sake of divine comedy
he dubbed the sound on afterwards,
and fashioned then the human ear
for the click of rapid heel on floor,
the silent-slamming door, the gadgetry
of tragicomedy, the *rhubarb*
of a babbling Babel; and so began
his gallant dance, the fingertip on satin strap
so as not to stroke the tender back,
so as not to intervene.

I'm from California Too

– Really? Which part?
All of me.

O frère du mal,
o brother in harms,
I forgive you –

for hiding your flea circus
in our bed for safekeeping,
then waking nonplussed
by the itching and scratching –

for letting us go hungry
for three whole days:
yesterday, today
and tomorrow –

for feeding me hard-boiled eggs and nuts
in my hospital bed,
then hanging my wet plaster cast
out to dry, five storeys high –

for planing the seat of my pants
clean off and making my butt
the butt of the joke once again
for my pains –

for signing me up for the Foreign Legion
where we fought to unforget
the thing you'd joined to forget
but forgot –

for assuring me that life isn't short enough,
which is why you've gone West
in your squashed-narrow car,
backfiring through the straight gates of Heaven,
without me as shotgun.

Pardon me,
my ear is full of milk.
There's something in my eye.

A Barren Moon

It's the one that Huygens hooked
like a duck
from the fairground game
of space.

Entitled *Titan* then,
child of The Golden Age,
terror of men,
closing breast to breast with Zeus,
snuffed out like a thunderbolt.

We had conclusive proof:
microbial life
beneath her clouds
and it fell to me
to prep the probe
and keep the instruments
free of all contaminants
for fear of harming
the alien spores.

Budding
organic
complexity.

Somehow a shred
of humanity
from underneath
my fingernail

splashed down
into her secret sea
and wiped them out.

Our brethren thread.
The second lightning strike
of Life – invisible meteorite.

The powers that be
Renamed the moon *Remorse*,
after me.

The Real Hands of a Thunderbird

I get by on my dimples, permafrown,
flytrap peepers, plugged-in hairline;
can bear the spinal fusion, lock-jawed joints,
my awkwardness at cocktail parties, jiving
to The Shadows, trying to ignore the shadows
of my strings strummed along the walls.

I'm a wizard in a fix, sure thing
in a shootout, dab hand at a ding-dong,
cool head in a jam: a safe pair of hands.

                    But it is my hands, father,
                    my hands: these pickers and stealers.

From a certain range they're fine,
good for yanking a joystick, hooking up a winch,
waving a pistol or sliding down rope
but when I bring them close

                    I see the grooveless pads
                    of palpable fingertip, the fleshy press and give,
                    the pores like sweaty spiracles, reminding me
                    of liquid life within, swirling the urges,
                    bathing hidden organs underneath
                    this scooped and scalloped plastic torso,
                    stiff civility, strict utility,
                    international usefulness.

And then I get the mischievous itch,
the pricking in the thumbs,

and my actions become opposable;
these digits want to do, do and do:
undo the sailor's knots of reputation,
unbutton, unzip, unveil, unsheathe,
undress, caress, explore whatever's underneath
Tin-Tin's dress.

                Distress calls me back to duty.
                Just once I'd like to let the kid plunge,
                the plane crash, the oil rig collapse.

East End Eel

Are you for real?
Are you the real deal?
Not jellied, not gelid, smooth-bellied.

How could you let me reel you in?
Do you not fear my keepnet creed, my creel?
Does your blood not congeal?

Are you conger or moray?
What are your social mores?
Could you power a flashlight?

I saw you flash in the light,
so maybe there's my answer –
yes-oh-yes.

Unswervingly you came to me
but let's make a deal:
you slip back,

give the English carp some old flannel,
suffer them to come unto me,
go peddle your snake oil downstream.

A Question of Obsession

Would you say you have a healthy obsess life?

Do you believe in obsess before marriage?

How do you keep your obsess life exciting?

Do you fantasise about obsess with strangers?

How old were you when you first had obsess?

Is obsess without love a shallow experience?

Do you have obsess outside the bedroom?

Have you ever had obsess in a car, on the street, in a cinema?

What's your most memorable obsess?

How do you feel about rough obsess?

Have you ever had obsess on a first date?

Would you ever pay for obsess?

Have you ever seen an obsess therapist?

Which celebrity would you most like to obsess with?

What's the kinkiest obsess you've ever had?

What's the obsessiest thing about you?

What makes someone obsessy?

Which of you tends to initiate obsess?

What do you do if your partner isn't interested in obsess?

How many times do you obsess per week?

Could you stay in a relationship without obsess?

Do you think obsess goes beyond the physical?

What's a normal amount to obsess?

Do you think you will ever obsess again?

Sandy's Carbon
i. m. Alexander Hutchison

Great stars die to make carbon –
it's an old story,
by now a banality,
a causal chain of
in-ev-it-a-bil-it-y
once set in motion,
once the stopwatch is started,
once the third-act countdown has begun,
once the information is passed,
hand-over-hand along the chain,
through the millions of compounds that carbon sustains,
delivering the message in powdery envelopes
that dust will have dust.

But that's not the point.

The point is that carbon makes brains,
fleeting tongues, fragile lungs
that billow for a day in the solar wind,
carrying breath beyond the probes of technology,
crafting golden discs not in factories
but in the irises of widening eyes,
armours the soul like a dutiful page,
puts flesh and blood and bone
on the idly doodled map of hopes
and fears and the ludicrous wish
to make a dance of this, to try new steps to this,
to waltz and tango and cha-cha and foxtrot
across the abyss and we need dancing masters like you
for this.

Treblinkium

Blink and you'll miss it.
A half-life of no life,
of one life, of all life.

When is a blink not a blink?
When the lids close their palms
and will not part.

If you time it right
you can blink out the truth,
stroboscope

the bad from the good,
see a droplet quiver
forever

and never drop.
What do you call a droplet
that doesn't drop?

A drop-not? A drop knot.
The trapdoor gapes
beneath your feet

but blink at the right rate
and you needn't see it.
History has a scent.

Discovered in 1942:
a scurfy residue,
an odour of Godlessness.

Occurs in nature, detectable
in little landslides
of shoes, spectacles,

fillings, wedding bands,
earrings clinging
to their lobes.

Let it decay,
blot it out,
blink it away.

Neptunal

Mother of all blues: twelve bar, low strung,
far flung. Eighth dot on the fret board, eight chords
from the broad sound hole of the sun.

Strum

Neptunal creatures hereabouts
open gentian eyes in dens when
the blue string thrums its darkling thing.

They breast the waves of indigo,
crest never-breaking swells that swamp horizons,
flood the heart and pluck the pluck

Sturm

from all of us. Father of the seas,
muster all your gravity to sift us,
stranding all our subtle strands in the lees.

No man is an island but all I see
are sand bars, steppingstones,
setting suns. We're done.

Strum

Drift on, move unseen, tug gently
at our dreams, leave your prints
on the surface tension of tears, corneas.

Drain Fly

Not since Sri Lanka have I been so genocidal.
A race of mosquitoes put to the words without mercy –
Dombey and Son smiting its doom around
a bug-infested room in Nattandiya.

Now a London bathroom has caught drain fly
and each morning the pristine porcelain
looks like a Hollywood casting call for butlers
shot from Francis Ford Coppola's helicopter.

The quick and the dead, the bad and the beautiful,
surviving or succumbing to the Vietnam of bleach,
of *Raid*, of duct-tape traps, of thumbscrews,
of double-edged handclaps.

The strange man upstairs who scuttles between
telly and the offie has had a slow leak all summer
and now I'm reaping his musty sown oats,
his six-legged legacy. Home is a killing jar.
England Made Me. England betrayed us all.

Womb

Did I gnaw my fingers and thumbs in the womb?
As anxiety grew with each subdividing bar,
each stop fluffed on the uilleann pipes of gestation.

The stir of the audience muffled through the membrane,
the glow from the lighting rig thumbing the eyeballs,
the proto-heart ticking like a mouse's metronome,
the phallic rap of baton on the music stand,
the final coughs of settling spectators,
the unrecognised key, the unmatchable tempo,
the missed cue, the spotlit tears, the bad reviews,
the dressing room that has seen it all before
and sloughs you out.

I would love to return to my mother's womb
but now that I know her, the thought is obscene.
Now that I know her.

I'd Like My Mum to Get Herself a Cat

I'd like my Mum to get herself a cat
that always lands on soft iambic feet.
Her terriers were too scrappy for me,
too keen on hunting silence to its lair
to rip apart the burrow where it made
its home and raised its young on secrecy.
And even if she loved it more than me
I shouldn't mind. Who could begrudge the purr

that welcomes her after my obsequies
are done and she has shut the lid upon
father, husband and now son? She will need
a little bristling attention, something
warm and needy to make a quiet fuss.
Come Dinah, come Pluto, come Pussums, come puss.

Iarnród Éireann

The Spanish–Italian border was dismantled overnight
and the next day rusting flatbeds, snakes of freight,
metal fatigued as fuck groaned into view, uncoiling wire,
pitching barriers, angle-grinding watchtowers and turrets
with migraine sparks, and the English–Nazi border was christened
with street parties of Rippers & Crippens & Mosleys & Haw-Haws.
My heart had long lapsed, too expensive to renew,
the biometrics broken down, but I had my mother's papers
and a code word she swaddled in lullabies now lost but not forgotten.
To Dublin, then! With McCabe the Assassin,
on one of the last helicopters out of Sigh Gone,
a DC-3 out of West Berlin, an old crate out of Silvertown,
wings and fuselage clogged by imperial sugar work,
a sticky crash-landing in the Liffey, doggy-paddling
down the Dodder till we found a wharf to gorge on gorgonzola
with grinning green teeth and a bottle of Burgundy
from a sommelier who left no reflection
as the mirror-food floated towards us.

Fade to black with matt glasses of Vantablack® Guinness,
the most profound material known to man,
pints of vertical carbon nanotube
horizontally aligned by the end of the day;
a substance so dark it would razor off Narcissus's fizog
and wear it to Carnivale; a liquid so dense
it sequesters a thousand millennia of shipwrecks
in a fleck of quantum foam; a gaze so unflinching
it could mine your deepest buried obscenities
and post them on the hymn board of every church in Ireland;
a drink so light-sapping your lips tingle with Hawking radiation

as you place the Kubrick monolith back onto the beermat.
And from its depths we conjured an extempore lament,
the gallows-dodging McCabe and I:

I hate it when people jump off the right bridge but land in the wrong river.
  I hate it when people take money from other nations but sell their loan words.
I hate it when the power of Christ compels wrapping paper.
  I hate it when you blanch at the thought of a feral hedgehog in the Langeudoc.
I hate it when rapacious lyricists eulogise Yorkshire womanisers.
  I hate it when people are devoted to pure, sky-fucking jouissance.
I hate it when men with wide ties don't share their sandwiches.
  I hate it when people invoice me at midnight.
I hate it when your ten euro looks like a grilled rasher.
  I hate it when people conflate a sausage crucifix with a breakfast get-out.
I hate it that Five Guys Named Moe on Grey Velvet *is not a giallo musical.*
  I hate it when you send me your annual syntax bill.
I hate it when they say the sun's death will seal a trade deal with Proxima Centauri.
  I hate it when the receipt number for ten Guinness is #13.

Deeper, then, sans McCabe, into the verdant vulvaland,
Iarnród Éireann from Dublino to Luimneach,
Intercity, a head full of Hell, INRI, Iron Nails Ran In,
with *Mercier and Camier* sharing my table,
all elbows and shanks, playing footsie with the sleepers,
buggering any gap with the bitching gab,
shuffling trips to the buffet car for miniatures
and sticking up the trolley for plasticated *Jamesons*.
What are trains but wormholes through weather?
What's a drinks trolley but a clattering CAT-scan
of your liver's livid inventory?
What are *Tayto*s but body bags for tuber leprosy?
I tried to read but trainshake breeds flies from the alphabet,
juddering runes using sandwiches as treadmills,

vomiting the small print of the universe we never read
but still click **Agree**. Raindrops try to board
but have such small hands they can't carry tickets.
They clamp themselves to the gritty windows,
limpet mines triggered long-distance by light.

Light sleep broken by the brakes at Limerick Junction
where I grab somebody's bag and nearly alight
with a second life, a counterfeit self.
A good time to switch points, change the tune,
find a new electron shell to bat about above my crib.
Hitting 50, I'm starting to fuse iron at the core,
can feel my organs turning over in their sleep,
hitting snooze on cell regeneration,
shouldering into flesh duvets to snatch an hour more.
My heart is scared to go out these days
for fear of who might be on the landing, on the stairs,
peeps through net curtains to see if the coast is clear.
It should be nailed beneath floorboards, telling tales
in the splintered dark with a murdered cat for company.
Maybe if I'd had children I would be braver of necessity?
My dad thought I was 'soft'. I just wanted to climb trees
and learn the constellations and stay above trouble.

Trolley-bag lugging over the Shannon
I think of my grandfather tipping my mother
from a currach into the chill swell
for her first swimming lesson. Apocryphal?
Perhaps, but I hear her splash, taste the weed
reaching down her green throat and plucking
the strings from the harp of her lungs,
stuffing sheets of lost music into a strongbox

bound with chains and burying them in the silt
to choke and rust. The Salmon of Wisdom
lashed past her face, flicking a thin cicatrix
with a fin of foresight but she misread the sign,
took it for a grinning muddy pike and in the labour
of unwisdom dropped me into the world
on the old maternal Yoni yo-yo.
Bouncing the baggage into the Strand Hotel
I'm bumped up to the 'executive floor' and a croissant on my pillow,
a Corby trouser press for my tongue or lingam,
a life-coach crouching on the foot of the bed.
Wake up in the boot of a car coasting bumps
on the way to Woodcock Hill Bog for a team-building day
of trust games, foraging and grave digging.
And then I'm really awake to Limerick rain tapping its metres
on business-class windows, straining for rhymes in the dusk.

On with leaky red shoes into monochrome drizzle
that falls like Anna Magnani onto neorealist cobbles.
A writer buys shoes every five years and these Doc Martens
have split from the miles, evolving gills on their bellies;
flounders, bottom-feeders, sand-hiders, muggers of crabs and hermits.
All the sodden way to the house my Mum was raised in,
pigeonhole for a hundred birthday cards, an address
hid to memory that the hand knows, the pen knows,
the ink imprints with its platelets and plasma.
One Christmas I forgot to write it down and just kissed
the envelope but the card found its way to my aunty's house.
What does Lacan say about letters always arriving?
He's an awful eejit! Sure, he doesn't know us from the sky above us, like.
What has Lacan to do with the peaty smell in the air?
My first taste of foreign soil, my second whiff

of the womb's perfume on a Möbius litmus strip
of Anglo-Irish, Irish-English, the whole clan
branded with an unbreakable lineage of freckles,
future sunburns, fading stigmata that bleed under UV,
flashmob the forearms to simulate Mediterranean tans,
that once had me scrubbing my cheeks with a pumice stone
and bleach so no teacher could ever ask me again,
'Were you sunbathing under a sieve?' Well,
welcome Limerick rain, seep through my insoles,
anoint my feet, trickle your peaty vortices into the wounds.

The gravelly drive, the pebbly portico,
refuge for umbrellas in the porch behind jewelled glass.
I squelch into view, am greeted by my uncle's voice,
an octave higher than you expect from a man
built like a Martello. My socks are dark, wet,
and drop onto the hall floor like stillborn moles.
'Holes in the shoes, is it? Is that what we've come to?
Is that where we're at now? Holes in the shoes?
Have you seen this, Breda? Holes in the shoes!'
'Well it's been very dry in London.' 'Holes in the shoes!'
Palpable disappointment in this Versailles of portraits
of my successful younger cousins with families and
high-powered jobs overseas. But they're not here.
I am. We are. Mother and sister and uncle and aunt,
herded together by my sudden wish
to see 'home' again at 50 before everything – if not already –
is too late. And I'm comfortable with my disappointments,
the shrivelling heads of past loves and lost chances
spiked around my hut in the heart of Kurtz's Congo.
Don't be surprised – there are kids from Bethnal Green
who can stare at rotting heads in plastic bins

and still play the next level of Candy Crush Saga.
The rain persists as Prosecco is popped and glitter from cards
gets into buttercream and my aunty gifts me Armani shave balm
and we make plans to meet her twin for lunch –
my other aunty who got lost in the choppy estuary,
couldn't clamber back on board, was drawn by the Shannon
out to sea. It's been after those girls forever.

Next day, rain gone, what passes for sun bungs up the river like gouache.
I gawp at an emerald green postbox as I wait on the corner for the sisters.
My sister, their sisters, the whole day devoted to this solar system of sisters.
This postbox is dressed for Saint Patrick's Day,
only lets Saint Paddy's Day cards slip like Baileys through its slit lips,
disgorges invoices, final demands, sympathy cards, *decrees nisi*,
turns all lettering, all typefaces, into green biro – that signature
of the delirious, the unjust, the psychotic, the visionary, the unacceptable,
the indefensible, the irresponsible, the energetic and indomitable.
Ever been stalked by a biro of purest green, for your sins?
Every nook and cranny where spores of words can drift and catch
and push their webby syntax overflows with self-supporting,
autofecundating moss. London postboxes are monarchists,
colonialists, tin soldiers, slavers, Beefeaters, blushes of shame.
They follow orders. It's time to order lunch.

Squeezed into a booth for a waft of the Amalfi coast on a Limerick high street,
the five of us twitch menus and whiff the ever-present Shannon.
My aunty's eyes float over the choices with the indifference of one
who has eaten enough over seven decades. What is it with all this food?
The buying, the prepping, the cooking, the serving, the eating,
the clearing, the washing, the crapping, the whole cavalcade
regurgitating itself a few hours later. For the love of God
can't you just let me feed on air, imbibe sunlight,

draw juice from the green of plants in the garden, let the insects spin
my dynamo as they flit past on their way to *their* next meal –
will the universe never be done with eating, will the black holes
never take off their bibs, lay down their knives and forks, their spoons,
skip a course, cut out carbs, fast, go on hunger strike?
I fell for a Slovene at first sight. She said she was a breatharian.
I took it for a joke, an aspiration, a sign that we sun lovers were soulmates
but I never saw a crumb pass the event horizon of her lips in eleven years.

n
o

s
p
a
g
h
e
t
t
i
f
i
c
a
t
i
o
n

I've been trying to fast but after a week the cravings are too intense
and I binge on my unrequited scraps till I'm sick

and swallowed by shame and can't get dressed.
What thuggish god stuffed his rubber tubes into Adam and Eve?

I think my aunty knows me.
There's a moment of alignment,
equilibrium, as her eye balances
on the beam, like a pill of air
in a spirit level. *Don't look left*
to the past. Don't look right
to the future. Let's hold this gaze
of present time, this airlock,
this quarantine pod, switch off
the tick-tock of loss, the fall
of cells through the hourglass
that links the quick and the dead;
quick, this bubble will burst but
while we're here, tell me
one thing from your life,
push one seed into the soil
of time, one tendril whose skein
unspools to the Beginning, tell me
what makes you you, pluck one spore
that was all yours: no parents,
no sisters, no husband, no children,
no nuns, no priests, no doctors,
no saints, no Gardaí, no pets,
no errands to run, nobody's needs
to shunt yours into the ditch.
 'So now –'

So begins Heaney's *Beowulf*, near as dammit,
and I'm cross-leggèd in a Yorkshire classroom,

the pose of a yogic skull and crossbones.
Dog-end of the day, a murdering cloud over dull West Nab
raining ashes of missing children on the moors.
The Canadian substitute teacher makes fresh popcorn.
As we stuff our Old-World mouths with untasted delights
she horripilates us with Grendel's attack on *Heorot*,
seizing thirty souls from sleep to roast them alive at home
and gorge on thighs, buttocks, livers, hearts, lips, eyeballs.
A Standard Fireworks shed explodes on the dissolve-line of the hill
and my best friend's sister loses two fingers
packing trays of *Roman Candles* and *Mine of Serpents*
into cardboard boxes for the newsagents of Huddersfield.
Each time I prised the tight square lid off a biscuit tin,
like cracking open a casket in *The Mummy*,
I thought I might find her charred fingers in the moulded plastic slot
where the *Bourbons* should be. Biscuits were lifebuoys
against the dread tides of night: one more cup of tea at 9 o'clock,
one more bribe to hoodwink mum and dad and stay up past the watershed
but more often than not I was sunk and lay in bed by a damp wall
trying not to notice the twisted faces in the wardrobe doors,
the grimaces of the damned in the tortoiseshell marbling
with its ghoulish reflections, tongues of hell, and melting monsters.
Nowhere was safe. Nowhere is safe. Grendel burst
into the classroom that numb November day.
Late gasp of the year. The sunsetting of childhood.

There was an escape tunnel under the Pennines,
Pied Piper clipping the tickets, the whole trip from taxi to train
through the dragon's lair of half-remembered steam
to Holyhead and Dún Laoghaire, land of licence plates red as Dracula's eyes,
fabled land of black hair, pale skin, blue stares, the model of my mother
on every street, in every shop, on every passing bus,

her likeness licensed for other women to use so I could be aroused
without the guillotine of tribal taboo rattling from amniotic skies.
Before landfall, the lurch of the ferry, the pulse of ocean's engine,
a vessel like a cliff, a floating border, a sentient iron island,
Geppetto's shark, Leviathan sifting cars and coaches like krill,
families and backpackers like plankton, dissolved in gastric rust
as we wait for rescue. Tilting and tipping stomachs, pipetting poisons,
mixing tinctures, trying to find the balance between bile and endeavour,
baleen and spleen, adventure and emetic, before spewing us onto alien shore,
scrabbling like sand crabs away from the sea, a film in reverse,
trying to shake off evolution from mechanical, sand-scraped limbs.

Sand is trying to eat the world. Tiny autonomous grinding teeth.
Drill bits, beautiful and strange under the microscope, like everything is.
Howard Hughes Senior hijacked the patent from nature, invented
the rotary tri-corn rock-drill bit that harnessed the rage of every cuckold
and incel to bore oil from the ground, blood from a stone.
This is how the universe looks but, with massive moon-manatee eyes,
fumbling fat-fingered frequencies, distended lenses of need and greed
and perpetual fear, we miss it all, can't reconcile reality and vision
as we clamber over the genocidal pile of the dead to get to Heaven.
Howard Hughes Junior in his screening room, corralled by pee,
haunted by the lips outside the door, the breaths outside the door,
the words outside the door. Doorknob like a virus, crowned with spikes
teething through the soft gums of the world, born not astride a grave
but into the mouth of the next nearest person, a phantastic egg
in the womb of the throat: smooth chrome one second,
puffer fish the next, shrapnelling blades into the body politic,
the body empathetic, the body pathétique, the sobbing adagio of being.

I was the first to make every movement the adagio.
Forget your marches, your waltzes, your dynamics, your tension,

your contrast, your variety, foie gras this diet of gloom,
button a tunic over your viola torso, your cello hips.
There was a time I piped at a more perilous pitch,
marching through slush-soddened streets with scraps of carols
pinched in a wonky lyre on a dinged and battered cornet –
Adeste Fideles; Stille Nacht, heilige Nacht,
Alles schläft, einsam wacht; There is a green hill
far away, without a city wall, where our dear Lord –

Drop thy pipe, thy happy pipe.
Drop thy spear, thy piercing spear.
Drop thy sponge, thy parching sponge.
The droghte of March hath perced to the roote.

So now – I'm home. Not *home* home, but *here* home.
A home withdrawn to its hole in the skirting board of history,
afraid of dinghies, of landings, invasions, glueing traps
for its monoglot tongue, gnawing off wishbone-thin limbs,
collecting a small pile of porous bones that will be melted
by snowflakes come winter. And winter is here and winter
is when I return, in new shoes, *Shoes for Life* – a lifetime guarantee,
a marketing spasm, that will shoe my feet into the grave, for free,
because a sister is gone, an aunty is lost, a plot hole revealed.

Back onto the Iarnród. Spare the rod and spoil the child.
But first my feet across Beckett's bridge, razor
through the optic nerve of the Liffey. Buñuelian architecture.
Orwell hated *La Sagrada Familia* but you can't be right all the time,
sometimes a mason's red-hot chip catches you in the throat.
Farewell to my familiars, Mercier and Camier, hello
to whomever's birth was the death of them – Baron Samedi
plunging the engine into Freudian tunnels of bubbling black mud,

a skeleton service, South by Southwest, rushing more
out of fear of being late for the start of the end
than from fear of the end beginning before I'm too late.
I'm back too soon. This was all supposed to be done and dusted,
the sacred family bonds piped close with caramel and tooth enamel.
The Tooth Fairy is a monster in her world, her cave strewn
with chap-fallen Act V gags, traces of gums. We're getting on,
there are no sixth acts in Anglo-Irish lives.

And so the long day closes, the road runs out, the buffers dissolve,
the sleepers separate like spliced DNA giving up the ghost.
The station was a green screen, the carriages CAD lines
in a blank simulation with no O-D matrix. We're astonied
to be gathered again. Cousins try to recognise each other
after decades of loving neglect, flick through the Rolodex
of buried anecdotes, blushing crushes, stitches and grazes
in the A&E department of contused memory.
I break the panopticon by smashing every mirror,
they piece me back together in the fragments of their eyes.
My dad crawls out of the ground and pleads for a piggy-back.
I carry him along with this coffin, this new weighty loss,
this hod-load of absent bricks that curves the spine and dislocates
the shoulder. Pallbearers sob. I've heard this sound before.
I watch my shoes. Black shoes. Black shoes tracking
from consecrated tile to municipal tarmac to patchwork pathway
to disturbed soil. Open up the ground again. Delve into the insects' world,
Earth felt the wound. Zounds! The last thing you need is a funeral.

I fly home from Shannon. When I was small, I thought the river was a runway
and planes splashed down and took off from dank hangars of weed.
She's gone. And Sionna has gone, leaving only her wisdom, which I fly from.
Goodbye Iarnród Éireann, goodbye Abhainn na Sionainne.

Notes, Touchstones & Translations

'San Bernardino'
There's a painting by Lorenzo Lotto.
I carried my secular soul here
To see the Madonna, the saints, the angels.

'Saint Teresa a Firenze'
Various adages and clichés, plus versions of speeches from Martin Luther King, John Fitzgerald Kennedy, Shakespeare's *Henry V, Ecclesiastes,* and *Genesis* (King James Version)

'After Baal's Hymn' and 'After Brecht's Hymn'
Inspired by David Bowie's performance in Bertolt Brecht's play *Baal* (BBC, 1982) and the EP of songs from the show. The former poem lifts a line from Samuel Taylor Coleridge's *The Rime of the Ancient Mariner.*

'Unextraordinary Light (for Euclid)'
A line lifted from Samuel Beckett's radio play *Embers.* For more information see: https://www.esa.int/esatv/Videos/2022/07/The_Fingertip_Galaxy_Reflecting_Euclid_in_art

'AAIANTRCTA'
The references to Jason and Talos are from Apollonius's *Jason and The Golden Fleece* and the classic film *Jason and the Argonauts.*

'Midlife Crisis'
There are no quotes but the spirit of Ben Jonson's 'To Penshurst' haunts this poem.

'Spomenik III: Eyebombs'
These phrases are suggested by the appearance of the postwar Yugoslavian monuments known as spomeniks (see https://www.spomenikdatabase.org).

'Orca Heart'
I hope readers recognise the film of *Jaws* and Quint's demise in this poem (in another poem he survives). The Heart poems add to a sequence begun in my book *Neptune Blue* (Salt, 2011).

'Shard Heart'
I can see this famous landmark from my windows. The brief snippet of Italian means 'What do you think?'

'Vertiginous – a Suite'
This multi-poet, multimedia performance at the British Film Institute also featured Mona Arshi, Dzifa Benson, Isobel Dixon, Chris McCabe and Chrissy Williams.

'Now Showing at The Corona'
References the following films, a sample of the hundreds I watched during
Covid lockdowns: *Aliens, Vertigo, Ringu, Death Walks at Midnight, Death
Walks on High Heels, The Aviator, King Kong, Taxi Driver, The Godfather, Jaws,
Portrait of a Lady on Fire, Melancholia, L'Eclisse*.

'La Genèse de M. Hulot (pour Jacques)'
Tati said: Let there be light! And there was light. This poem references Jacques
Tati's three masterpieces, *Les Vacances de Monsieur Hulot, Mon Oncle*, and
Playtime.

'I'm from California Too'
This poem is chiefly inspired by Laurel and Hardy's classics *Sons of the Desert,
Hog Wild, One Good Turn, County Hospital, Beau Hunks, Busy Bodies*, and *Way
Out West*.

'The Real Hands of a Thunderbird'
I have always been mildly disturbed by the real human hands they used in
close-up shots on this puppet show.

'Drain Fly'
This poem references Graham Greene's *England Made Me* and Black Box
Recorder's song of the same name.

'I'd Like My Mum to Get Herself a Cat'
The cats in the final line come from *Alice in Wonderland* (Lewis Carroll), *The
Black Cat* (Edgar Allan Poe) and *Ulysses* (James Joyce).

'Iarnród Éireann'
The poem is configured around two triangular trips between London, Dublin
and Limerick. The first trip was planned and long overdue, the second trip
following hard on its heels at the behest of an unexpected funeral. It is a tale
of (the) red shoes and black shoes and a marketing promise of 'Shoes for Life'
that has since been withdrawn.

The Spanish–Italian border is a joke of mine that poet Róisín Tierney turned
into an excellent poem and book called *The Spanish–Italian Border* (Arc
Publications, 2014). Here the imaginary border returns under crisis.

McCabe the Assassin is a character from Samuel Beckett's story 'Dante and
the Lobster'. It's also my nickname for the poet Chris McCabe. The block of
italicised lines was extemporised by Chris and I in a pub in Dublin the day
before my 50th birthday. The Assassin has given his permission for some of his
words to be reproduced.

Leo Bloom's lunch of a Gorgonzola sandwich with Burgundy at Davy Byrne's
pub (*Ulysses* by James Joyce, 1922).

Is Guinness black or red? I experience it, phenomenologically, as black but apparently it is deep red (*Profondo Rosso*?).

'Iron Nails Ran In': these nails are extracted from *Ulysses*.

Mercier and Camier by Samuel Beckett (written in 1946, published in 1970).

Taytos: legendary potato crisps.

'somewhere i have never travelled, gladly beyond' by e.e. cummings (1931).

The Salmon of Knowledge: a mythic creature that dwells in the Boyne River. I have lured it from its usual waters.

Rome, Open City (Roberto Rossellini, 1945).

Heart of Darkness by Joseph Conrad (1899).

Yoni: a Sanskrit word that has been interpreted to mean the womb and the female organs of generation.

Beowulf (700–1000 AD).

Beowulf: A New Verse Translation by Seamus Heaney (1999).

Pinocchio by Carlo Collodi (1883).

Spaghettification is the process by which (in some theories) an object would be stretched and ripped apart by gravitational forces while falling into a black hole.

The Aviator (Martin Scorsese 2004).

Waiting for Godot by Samuel Beckett (1953).

6th Symphony by Pyotr Ilyich Tchaikovsky (1983).

George Orwell: 'For the first time since I had been in Barcelona I went to have a look at the cathedral – a modern cathedral, and one of the most hideous buildings in the world.' (*Homage to Catalonia*, 1938).

Songs of Innocence and Experience by William Blake (1789).

The Canterbury Tales by Geoffrey Chaucer (1387–1400).

Baron Samedi: played by choreographer Geoffrey Holder in *Live and Let Die* (Guy Hamilton, 1973). His final scene fuses interestingly with *North by Northwest* (Alfred Hitchcock, 1959).

Endgame by Samuel Beckett (1957).

Paradise Lost by John Milton (1667).

Sionna: the river goddess of the Shannon, renowned for her beauty and cunning.

Acknowledgements & Thanks

'Divine Hours' was published in *Spark: Poetry and Art Inspired by the Novels of Muriel Spark*, edited by Rob A. Mackenzie and Louise Peterkin (Blue Diode Press, 2018) and is a response to Spark's novel *The Abbess of Crewe*.

'San Bernardino' and 'Santa Teresa a Firenze' were written for, and performed at, the inaugural Festival of Italian Literature (FILL) in London in 2017. The event was devised by Livia Franchini.

'Unextraordinary Light (for Euclid)' was written to accompany Lisa Pettibone's artwork 'Fingertip Gallery', 2023. Both artwork and poem are currently on board the European Space Agency's spacecraft Euclid, as it hunts for dark matter.

'Vampire in the Funhouse, Part I' was published in *Deleuzine* volume 2, 2023.

'On the Care and Handling of Seas' was written for *Lookout: Poetry from Aldeburgh Beach*, edited by Tamar Yoseloff (Lookout Editions, 2017).

'AAIANTRCTC' was written for the occasion of the 'AntartiCA55 Expedition to the 7th Continent', January 2020. It was a highly commended poem in the Ginkgo Prize for Ecopoetry, 2020.

'Polar Heart' was written for the RSA's *Seven Dimensions of Climate Change* event series, 2015.

'Spomenik I–V' were written as part of Creative Commissions: Mobility Variations, supported by the Centre for GeoHumanities, Royal Holloway University and the Centre for Advanced Studies in Mobility with the Department of Historical and Geographical Sciences and the Ancient World, University of Padova. There is poetry-film version of 'III: Eyebombs' on Vimeo at https://vimeo.com/495784595.

'Spomenik II: Found Nostalgia' is adapted from the online article 'How Quickly Will Water Damage Ruin Your Home?' at www.waterdamagemiami.com

'Absinthe Punch in Bratislava' was published in *Slovakia in Poems*, edited by Elena Cay (Global Slovakia, 2021).

'Vertiginous': My poems from the multi-poet, multimedia performance at the British Film Institute. The event also featured Mona Arshi, Dzifa Benson, Isobel Dixon, Chris McCabe and Chrissy Williams.

'Now Showing at The Corona' was broadcast on BBC Radio 4's Covid locked down (and now sadly defunct) *Film Programme* on July 9, 2021.

'ALIEN Dream Song' was published in *Berryman's Fate: A Centenary Celebration in Verse*, edited by Philip Coleman (Arlen House, 2014).

'A Portrait of ALIEN as a Young Man' was published as part of the Afterword in *Alien (BFI Film Classics)*, by Roger Luckhurst (British Film Institute, 2014).

'thou sHALt' was published in *Split Screen*, edited by Andy Jackson (Red Squirrel Press, 2012).

'La Genèse de M. Hulot (pour Jacques)' was published in *Double Bill*, edited by Andy Jackson (Red Squirrel Press, 2014).

'I'm from California Too' was first published in *Magma 66, Comedy* Issue, 2016.

'A Barren Moon' and 'The Real Hands of a Thunderbird' appeared in the anthology *When Rockets Burn Through*, edited by Russell Jones (Penned in the Margins, 2012).

'East End Eel' was published in *The Creel*, an anthology about eels, edited by LukeThompson (Guillemot Press, 2018). There is a poetry-film version of it on Vimeo at https://vimeo.com/507604433.

'Treblinkium' was published in *Under the Radar 28*, 2001/2002.

'Neptunal' was published in *Magma 56*, 2012.

'Drain Fly' was published in Chrissy Williams's webzine *Perverse*, 2019.

'Iarnród Éireann' was previously published as a standalone pamphlet by Broken Sleep Books, 2021.

Thank you to Isobel Dixon, Chris McCabe, Christopher Reid, Roisin Tierney, Luke Heeley, Liane Strauss, John Canfield, Pinuccia Vianini, Elisa Bormida, Roger Luckhurst, Dilantha Goonetillake, Jack Wake-Walker, Ollie Barrett, James Riding, Lisa Pettibone, Tom Kitching, Kat Austen, Andre Bagoo and Aaron Kent.

LAY OUT YOUR UNREST

www.ingramcontent.com/pod-product-compliance
Lightning Source LLC
Chambersburg PA
CBHW030850090426
42737CB00009B/1179